Deep in the Amazon

RAINFOREST RESEARCHERS

A short-tailed fruit bat, a resident of the understory, approaches a bird-of-paradise flower. Here the bones, membranes, and blood vessels that make up the wings stand out in fine detail showing how perfectly adapted this group of mammals is to an aerial life.

Deep in the Amazon

RAINFOREST RESEARCHERS

by James L. Castner

BENCHMARK BOOKS

MARSHALL CAV
NEW YOR

SOUTHERN
OKLAHOMA
Library System
Ardmore, Oklahoma

CHICKASAW REGIONAL LIBRARY
ARDMORE, OKLAHOMA

MAR 50993

With thanks to Dr. Gary Hartshorn, Organization for Tropical Studies,
Duke University, for his careful review of the manuscript.

Benchmark Books
Marshall Cavendish Corporation
99 White Plains Road
Tarrytown, New York 10591-9001
www.marshallcavendish.com

• • •

Library of Congress Cataloging-in-Publication Data
Castner, James L.
Rainforest Researchers / by James L. Castner
p. cm. — (Deep in the Amazon)
Includes bibliographical refernces (p.) and index.
ISBN 0-7614-1129-1
1. Rain forests—Research—Amazon River Region—Juvenile literature. [1. Rain forests—Research. 2. Amazon River Region.] l. Title.

QH112 .C372 2001   578.734'0981'1—dc21   00-069909

• • •

Printed in Hong Kong
1 3 5 7 8 6 4 2

• • •

Book Designer: Judith Turziano
Photo Research: Candlepants Inc.

• • •

CREDITS
Cover photo: Paul Donahue and Teresa Wood
The photographs in this book are used by permission and through the courtesy of;
Animal Animals: Stephen Dalton, OSF, title page, 19; Thompson D. OSF, 20; Earth Scenes,
Robert Lubeck, 34; Barbara Von Hoffmann, 56. *Photo Researchers*: Gregory G. Dimijian,
8, 28, 36; Don Goode, 13; Merlin D. Tuttle, 16(bottom), 21, 22; Gary Rutherford, 26(top);
Margie Politzer, 26(bottom); Pascal Goetgheluck/Science Source Library, 29; Renee Lynn, 37;
Kjell B. Sandved, 47. *Peter Arnold*: BIOS (M. Gunther), 10. *Dr. James L. Castner*: 12, 14, 40, 42.
Don Wilson: 16(top). *Jim Duke*: 24, 30. *Gary Hartshorn*: 32, 38. *Terry Erwin*: 43, 44.
Paul Donahue and Teresa Wood: 48, 50, 54. *Corbis*: Eric and David Hosking, 53.

CONTENTS

CARIBBEAN SEA

ATLANTIC OCEAN

VENEZUELA

GUYANA

SURINAME

FR. GUIANA

COLOMBIA

ECUADOR

PERU

BRAZIL

BOLIVIA

PARAGUAY

CHILE

URUGUAY

ARGENTINA

PACIFIC OCEAN

0   400 miles

0   600 kilometers

Research Sites

(locations are approximate)

Don Wilson

Jim Duke

Gary Hartshorn

Terry Erwin

Paul Donahue & Teresa Wo

AUTHOR'S NOTE

For some people, going to work means trudging down a muddy trail, and the "office" consists of the millions of acres that make up the tropical rain forests of the Amazon Basin. These people are scientists. More specifically, they are tropical biologists, and their studies involve the wide range of life that calls the rain forest home. You might find them marking wasps with paint, capturing bats in wispy nets, or sketching a bird from a walkway built high in the trees.

Clearly, their studies and experiments could never take place in an office. Instead, they must put themselves in the middle of the action, in the heart of the Amazon region.

It is not for everyone. But to these dedicated scientists, the rewards are great. Their important work helps us to better understand and protect the rain forests of South America.

We are about to meet six of these hearty and curious folks. Over the course of their studies, they have grown to love the rain forest and to think of it as their second home. There is always something new to be learned here. Maybe one day you too can unlock some of the mysteries of this fascinating world.

Tropical rain forests are among the most challenging places to work. A cloud forest, such as this one lying at an elevation of about 1 mile (1,700 m), may force the visitor to wear a jacket or extra layers to avoid the cold and damp.

Chapter One

THE BASICS

W orking in the Amazon rain forest is often difficult, but it is always rewarding. There are still isolated areas that have yet to give up their secrets. Not long ago, a new species of primate was discovered outside of Sao Paulo, Brazil. The researcher credited with this new find had logged years of study and field work before he made such a rare and important discovery. So although it is often hard work, it does offer the potential of making a lasting contribution to the world of science.

Rainforest research presents challenges that test both your mental and your physical fitness. To make the most of working in a rain forest, a broad background in the natural sciences is essential. My own training is in entomology—the study of insects—with a lesser focus on botany—the study of plants. Yet how many times have I wished I knew much more about the forests' other creatures? They too interact with the plants and insects I study. Walking along a forest trail at night with a headlamp, I often see a variety of frogs and snakes. Yet it has taken me years to be able to identify them. When it comes to the rain forest, you could never learn too much to help you in your work.

Clearly, to be a rainforest researcher requires a great deal of scientific preparation. But that is not all. There are qualities we all share that help make a top-notch investigator. Curiosity, patience, and the ability to be a sharp observer are essential. You probably won't be an effective student of the rain forest if you don't have a great interest in your work. Many times

Jane Goodall's persistence was rewarded when her constant presence
was finally accepted by the wild chimpanzees she was studying.
Her work revealed a whole new world about chimpanzee behavior
that was only made possible through her field observations.

during my travels in the Amazon, I have noticed that the people who knew the most have not been the ones with the greatest number of science degrees, but those who were passionate about the organisms they studied.

Most important field work begins by simply watching the subjects you're studying and the world in which they live. Many animals are wary and difficult to approach. Jane Goodall spent years gaining the confidence of the chimpanzees with which she worked. Many researchers do most of their observing through binoculars. They spend long hours trying to identify animals that are partially hidden in leafy trees or energetically hopping from branch to branch. Such work can be frustrating and requires a great deal of patience.

In other cases, the object of the study may be easy to see but difficult or dangerous to observe closely. At the beginning of my career, I worked as an Earthwatch volunteer, studying the behavior of tropical wasps. Much of my time was spent on a ladder, with my face less than a foot away from the wasp nest. It was uncomfortable and more than a little nerve racking. Marking these live wasps with paint and then releasing them was even more of a challenge. Yet it is an essential part of a mark-recapture study. Marking helps researchers identify an individual organism and thus study its behavior over a long period of time.

Perched on the ladder painting wasps, I first realized another important quality a researcher must possess—the ability to adapt to the world around you. And when it comes to the Amazon Basin, that world can be downright hostile. In order to study katydids, I have spent many hours at night walking along rainforest trails. Along the way, I have been bitten or stung by mosquitoes, ants, wasps, caterpillars, and even a couple of plants. I have nearly stepped on or grabbed several poisonous snakes. At times I have spent the entire night with field assistants seated on a small wooden stool watching katydids through red-filtered lights. Even doing something you love takes persistence when hundreds of mosquitoes are buzzing around you.

Then there's the climate. And the terrain. The heat and the humidity of the rain forest can be especially nasty foes. They sap your strength and threaten dehydration. And although I typically work in lowland rain forests, the rugged terrain of the Andes Mountains can make walking very difficult. Although well-equipped camps and workstations do exist, many rainforest researchers find themselves far from the comforts of home. When out in the field, you often need to rely entirely on the supplies and equipment you have brought with you.

Finally, there is a valuable, if often overlooked, resource that could provide a researcher with a wealth of information—the people who live in the region in which you are working. But if you are studying birds or bats or katydids, how could the native inhabitants be of any assistance? Most

As part of a mark-recapture study, a katydid is indentified with a dab of paint and a label with a number on it. This is done so that, when a researcher observes its behavior, the insect is not confused with other members of its species.

When biologists gain the trust and respect of the local people,
they often accomplish their goals more quickly and easily.
This native inhabitant lives in eastern Panama.

of the people of the Amazon Basin have lived there for their entire lives. They know the place they call home as well as its plants and animals very well. Being able to communicate with these locals is essential. Whether it is Spanish, Portuguese, or a local dialect you have to learn, these people almost always have something to share. Just like a good researcher, they are keen observers too and can offer insight into the behavior and habits of the subject you are studying. After all, they are part of the vast web of connections that bind all the region's living things.

So who are some of these people so passionate about rainforest life they have chosen to study it as their career? What are some of the things they research and how, exactly, do they go about it? Let us take a look at just a few of the dedicated scientists, researchers, and naturalists who have contributed to our understanding of tropical forest communities.

Don Wilson and a Peruvian colleague below are about to enter the forest to set up mist nets at a field site in northeastern Peru. Biologists who focus on nocturnal creatures must often do double duty. They prepare traps and equipment during daylight hours and capture and study the animals after dark.

Chapter Two

BAT MAN

*D*r. Don Wilson has a passion for bats. As a mammalogist—a scientist who studies mammals—he has spent his career examining the biology and behavior of bats. Now, as a senior scientist with the Smithsonian Institution's National Museum of Natural History in Washington, D.C., he is especially interested in studying how these unique mammals interact with other plants and animals.

Bats are fascinating creatures. However they are not the easiest animals in the world to study. In fact, their nocturnal habits, secretive nature, and ability to fly make them one of the most difficult animals to observe. Bats are such agile aviators that special methods are needed to capture them. To collect his subjects, Don uses what bat researchers have relied on for decades—a mist net.

The mist net is an extremely fine, nearly invisible, lightweight nylon net. It measures roughly 7 feet (2.1 m) high and can range from 20 to 60 feet (6–18 m) long. When stretched out and held up by poles on either end, it presents a surface area of 140 to 420 square feet (13–39 sq m). But the mist net has proved most effective when it is placed across a likely flight path of foraging bats. It takes an experienced and sharp-eyed mammalogist to identify these possible routes.

While many species use a type of sonar or echolocation to find their insect prey, these high-pitched sounds the bats send out do not detect the net. Thus bats will fly straight into the light, springy material and become all tangled up. Don and his colleagues then need to remove the small

As part of his work, mammalogist Don Wilson (left) has collected bats from around the world. Here he is shown with Jorge Salazar displaying bat specimens that were captured at a field site in Bolivia.

Here two scientists free a bat that is tangled in a mist net. These large and nearly invisible nets are very effective in capturing bats and sometimes also birds.

struggling balls of fur, teeth, and knotted nylon. The distressed bats often chatter and cry out to express their displeasure at being snared. Untangling an agitated bat is not easy.

Bats turn their insect meals into energy at a rapid rate. By flying and foraging, they burn this energy quickly. So the ones that are captured must be removed right away, or they will die of exposure. Carefully and gently, each of the small mammals is untangled until it is free. Then the bat can be measured and examined and the various data recorded. A pair of leather gloves is a wise precaution against the small, sharp teeth of most species. Most bat researchers also prepare themselves with a series of rabies shots to guard against the possibility that some of the bats they handle may carry the disease.

Leaf-Nosed Flyers

Sometimes there is only a gaping hole left in the mist net. Most likely one of the larger, more aggressive species has torn its way completely through. In the Amazon Basin, there are approximately one hundred species of bats. Most only have a wingspan of 12 inches (30.4 cm) or less and weigh no more than a few ounces. However, the spectral bat — *Vampyrum spectrum*, also known as the false vampire bat—is a large predator. It searches for roosting birds and small mammals. It may have a wingspan as large as 3 feet (0.9 m) and weigh up to half a pound (226 g). It often roosts in hollow trees, around the base of which may be scattered the bones, skulls, and other grisly remains of past meals.

The spectral bat belongs to the group or family of bats called the *Phyllostomidae*, commonly known as the leaf-nosed bats. They get their name from the fact that their nose is shaped like a large flap or "leaf." This unusual structure acts as a megaphone to amplify the sounds used as sonar. These sounds are made through the nose and are typically beyond the range of human hearing. The bats can hear them however, and know whether a sound bounced off an object indicates an insect, a tree branch, or another bat. In addition, leaf-nosed bats tend to have broad wings, which allow them to fly slowly and with great precision. This ability is essential in pursuing and capturing their insect prey, which is often snatched directly off foliage rather than taken from the air in midflight.

However, in the case of the spectral bat, it is not tiny moths and insects that are sought. *Vampyrum spectrum* is the top carnivore among the New World bats. In the wild it will feed on other bats, birds, and rodents. In captivity it has been known to eat frogs, lizards, and even large insects. On several occasions, Don has captured both a male and female at the same time, suggesting that this species may forage together during the night. Teamwork seems to play a role in the lives of spectral bats. The females give birth to only one offspring per year and along with their mates they care for the young by bringing food back to the roost for it. They often live in family groups that consist of one adult breeding pair and several other juvenile bats.

Mutual Support

In some cases bats feed directly on the fruits of certain trees. Although local farmers may become upset, the bats are actually playing an important role. They disperse the seeds of the parent tree. The plant world often relies on, and goes out of its way to attract, birds and mammals to transport seeds to a new habitat. In extreme cases, seeds will not even germinate and grow unless they have passed through the digestive system of a particular animal. One species, the Jamaican fruit bat, disperses literally millions of fig seeds throughout the Amazon Basin.

Fruit eating, or frugivory, is a special feeding habit typical of many species of leaf-nosed bats. Such bats are critical to rainforest ecosystems. Their seed dispersal services have resulted in the coevolution of some species of plants and bats. As a result the plants develop a syndrome known as chiropterophilly, or bat love. The symptoms of this syndrome include fruit that is fleshy and sweet, but not particularly strong smelling

Bats with broad wings, such as this false vampire bat, are able to
fly slowly and maneuver with great agility. These skills are especially
useful when bats thread their way among the rainforest foliage.

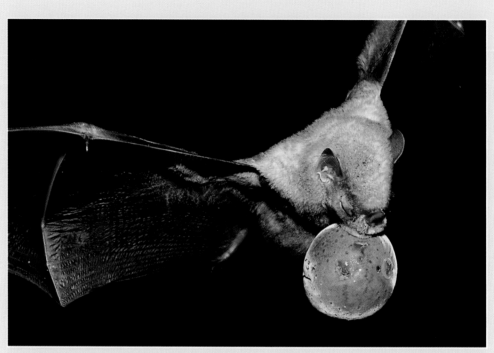

The big-eyed bats are a subgroup of the neotropical fruit bats.
Once a bat finds a fruit, it flies off with it to a feeding roost where
the meal is consumed. This one is on its way to eat a fig.

or colorful. The fruit often hangs down from parallel branches, so it is easy for the bats to access. These adaptations are all designed to attract the nighttime flyers. As a result, the small seeds are spread throughout the environment as the bat deposits waste in the course of flying to and from fruit-bearing trees and its roosting site.

Bats that feed on nectar and pollen are equally important to their rainforest home. Bats are responsible for pollinating an enormous number of plants. They aid tropical rain forests in all stages of development. Many of these nectar-feeders are again species of plyllostomids, or leaf-nosed bats. These flower-feeding bats have long muzzles and tongues that are covered

A nectar-feeding bat hovers in front of a banana flower, dipping its long red tongue into the sweet liquid. The slender tongue fits perfectly into the tubular blossom.

Bats help transfer pollen. When they stick their heads in
a flower to reach the nectar, their faces often become covered
with the dusty substance. This flying fox's face is
speckled with light-colored grains of pollen.

with fine bristles. These adaptations are especially useful for getting to the nectar and carrying away pollen at the same time.

Just like the plants that depend on bats for seed dispersal, the flowers that bats help pollinate have found their own special ways to attract them. Bat-pollinated flowers have qualities that are similar to those seen in bat fruits—pale or no colors and little to no fragrance. They also open at night rather than the day as is the case with flowers pollinated by insects or birds. The bats of Central and South America typically locate trees by using their sonar, then zero in on ripe fruits and open flowers by using their sense of smell. The flowers tend to be large, offering easier access to the tempting nectar inside. As the bat thrusts its head into the blossom, its fur becomes covered with a dust of pollen, which is then carried on to the next flower, pollinating it in the process. Among those trees that use bats for pollen transfer are the balsa, banana, and silk cotton or kapok trees.

Don's work on bat biology and ecology has brought to light some interesting facts and behaviors. In studies of bat reproduction, Don found that many species of tropical bats breed twice per year. In forested areas their cycles are closely tied to rainfall patterns. Many areas of tropical forest have both a long and short rainy season each year. The bats take advantage of the wealth of flowers, fruits, and insects that follow the rains to feed their young.

Nothing in the rain forest happens in isolation. Things that might seem unimportant, such as the pattern of rainfall or the size and color of a flower, affect other creatures immensely. Even though many people never see them, bats are an important part of their world. The seed scattering and pollination services these nocturnal fliers provide allow the forest to spread and thrive. Bats also help it recover by aiding new growth in areas that have been cleared or destroyed. Both carnivores and frugivores, both predators and prey, some of the secrets of bat behavior are now being revealed through the efforts of scientists like Don Wilson.

Jim Duke (right) and Peruvian colleague
Rodolfo Vasquez stand in the ReNuPeRu
Medicinal Plant Garden outside of Iquitos,
Peru. They are holding the leaves of a young
tree called vismia. The orange latex of this
plant is used throughout the Amazon
Basin to treat sores and wounds.

Chapter Three

THE GREEN PHARMACIST

D r. Jim Duke is not your typical scientist. This guitar-strumming botanist is known for walking barefoot through the rain forest in pursuit of his leafy subjects. He is one of the world's leading experts on medicinal plants. Jim spent thirty-five years working for the U.S. government, charged with finding out all he could about plants that could help people. This is the job of an economic botanist. But Jim was able to explore more than one facet of botany. For him, it is more than just the study of plants.

Jim is trained in plant taxonomy, the classification of different species. Without a system to organize plants and other organisms into separate categories, we wouldn't be able to identify them or tell the various species apart. In classifying the many plants he studies, Jim needs to be well versed in the procedures of a field botanist. This includes the proper manner in which to collect, dry, press, mount, and label specimens for entry into an herbarium. An herbarium is a type of museum that houses collection of plants. It is like a library for plants. The specimens are organized according to the category to which they belong. They serve as a vast reference collection to which samples of unknown plants may be compared in order to find out what they are.

While working at the Missouri Botanical Garden in St. Louis—one of the world's leading herbariums—Jim even discovered a new Amazonian plant. He named this genus *Sanango*, the Spanish name by which the

A Peruvian curandero (left), or healer, prepares herbal medicines from plants harvested in the rain forest. In his left hand are segments of the well-known cat's claw vine.

In a Bolivian marketplace (below), as well as throughout Latin America, one finds vendors of medicinal herbs in the local market. Stems, leaves, flowers, fruits, and pieces of bark are all sold for their medicinal value.

plant was commonly known in Peru. Jim has long believed that the best guide to plants is not a book, but the local people. He has had great success in befriending the native inhabitants of the regions in which he has worked. He asks them how they use the local plants and shares his own knowledge as well.

Jim spent nearly six years living with some of the peoples of the rain forest. He passed his time learning from the Kuna and the Choco of Panama and the Mahuna and Yagua of Peru. As he lived with these various ethnic groups, he closely observed and recorded their use of and dependence on forest plants and products. These groups had firsthand knowledge of medicinal plants and were using them on a daily basis. Through talking with local medicine men and shamans, Jim heard about the plant called cat's claw.

Jim first came in contact with the popular cat's claw vine while he was working in Panama in the 1960s. There, it was referred to as *bejuco de agua*, or the "water vine," as cutting it open and holding it to your mouth yields a drink of water. The common name of cat's claw comes from the paired clawlike tendrils that grow along the stem and allow it to climb into the canopy. Today, cat's claw is one of the best-known rainforest medicinal plants. It is sold in several forms in health food stores around the world. Its use is linked with stimulating the immune system. Thus it is taken for many different illnesses as well as a medicine that prevents the onset of sickness.

As an economic botanist, part of Jim's job was to evaluate the nutritional value of different plants. In the early 1970s, working with ethnobotanist Wade Davis, he performed an analysis on a sample of leaves sent to him from Bolivia. It came from a plant that was consumed daily by millions of people in South America. The lab results showed that the plant had an amazing variety of beneficial properties. It contained above-average quantities of vitamins, minerals, and calories. The amount of calcium was also higher than for any other edible plant. This fact alone

Coca leaves have been chewed by Andean Indians for thousands of years, long before the plant was used to produce the drug cocaine. Jim Duke was one of several researchers who analyzed the nutritional content of the leaves, revealing their many helpful properties.

showed the plant could be of great value—especially for nursing mothers—in an area such as the Andes where dairy products are scarce.

The sample leaves of this nutritious superplant had come from the coca bush. They were the same leaves that could be processed with chemicals to produce the drug cocaine. South American Indians had cultivated this plant and chewed its leaves for thousands of years with no ill effects. In fact, as Jim proved, it was obviously beneficial. Jim found that eating this plant every day more than met the Recommended Daily Allowance (RDA) for a large number of nutritional elements. The leaves not only serve as a food but as a mild stimulant that greatly helps people adapt to and tolerate living at high elevations. It also reduces feelings of hunger and increases energy and stamina.

In the past ten years, Jim has traveled to nearly fifty countries in South America, Asia, Africa, and the Middle East. He continues to study and

Botanists in Guyana collect plant specimens for an herbarium. There is still much to be learned from the countless species that are found in the Amazon Basin.

Jim Duke (right) translates for Peruvian shaman and healer Antonio Montero Pisco, as he addresses a group of North American tourists in the Peruvian Amazon. Jim has worked with many native experts to present field courses and workshops for both tourists and health-care workers from around the world.

lecture about medicinal plants, often working with those involved with the health profession. One of his current goals is to gain wider acceptance for alternative medications, such as herbs and plants, in the United States. He points out that many people in poorer countries, as well as 20 percent of those in the United States, cannot afford to purchase the medicines their doctors prescribe.

While Jim has traveled and worked throughout South America, much of his teaching and conservation efforts have centered on the Upper Amazon.

He has made forty-three trips to Peru to date and even established a medicinal plant garden outside of Iquitos with the help of Explorama Tours and the Amazon Center for Environmental Education and Research. Called the ReNuPeRu Garden, it contains more than three hundred medicinal rainforest plants and herbs used in the Upper Amazon. Carefully tended by a *curandero*, or native healer, the ReNuPeRu Garden serves as a wonderful teaching tool for those fortunate students who study with Jim in the field.

Today Dr. Jim Duke continues to share his knowledge with those who, like him, wish to explore the ways plants can benefit people. He is accepted by both medical doctors and local shaman, capable of speaking with each in their own language. His studies have unlocked the hidden properties of plants. He has shown how beneficial they can truly be. By proving the medical value of rainforest plants, Jim has provided yet one more reason why it is so important to preserve tropical forests.

Gary Hartshorn, tropical forester and conservationist, has spent most of his career learning about the rain forest. He is currently director of the Organization for Tropical Studies, a group of institutions responsible for training tropical biologists.

Chapter Four

THROUGH THE TREES

D r. Gary Hartshorn is the president of the Organization for Tropical Studies (OTS), a group that has helped provide training and field experience to countless tropical biologists. As an ecologist, he knows how essential this exposure can be. Gary's work focuses on tropical forests and the natural history of their trees. Early in Gary's career his research centered on studying the ecological life history of a single dominant species. That means finding out the role a species plays in the forest community, including how it grows, what pollinates its flowers, and what animals eat its seeds. Gary reasoned that by understanding the role of the dominant tree species he would gain a clearer understanding of the entire forest with its hundreds of other species. And as it turns out, Gary was exactly right.

For six years Gary studied the 1,384-acre (560-ha) forest of the La Selva Biological Station in Costa Rica. He became an expert on the dominant tree of this forest, a member of the mimosa family called gavilan. This tree was virtually everywhere at La Selva, found in 95 percent of the forest. When mature, it can reach a height of 115 feet (35 meters) and because it is so widespread, it forms the base of the canopy, or uppermost, layer of the forest. Gary's work has revealed some new facts about this species. For example, moths are mostly responsible for pollinating the flowers. The seeds contain chemicals that make them toxic to other seed-eating animals such as parrots and squirrels. The large seeds are more than 1

Light is an extremely important part of life in the rain forest.
Here along the edges of a stream in the La Selva forest, light levels
are high and result in the wild growth of shrubs, vines, and trees.

inch (2.5 cm) long and float, which is probably the main way they are dispersed throughout the wet forest. The result is nearly 100 percent germination, and often the floor of the forest is covered in a carpet of gavilan seedlings. Gary found that the gavilan had a fairly stable population, ranging from the occasional large, older trees to many medium-sized trees to a wealth of saplings and seedlings. The gavilan's toxic seeds along with its ability to tolerate wet conditions are two of the reasons it is so successful as a species.

One of the great scientific mysteries of tropical rain forests such as La Selva is how so many tree species can live together in a single place. Through his research, Gary was able to show how successful gavilan was as the dominant tree species in the La Selva forest. But if gavilan is such an adaptable tree, why has it not been able to totally dominate the La Selva forest? And what about the other trees that have trouble competing with gavilan for space? These trees have been forced to turn to tree fall gaps—patches in the forest where one or more large trees have fallen down. While identifying hundreds of tree species in La Selva, Gary noticed that saplings of some species are found only in these gaps.

By chance, some abandoned pastureland was added to the original La Selva property. While walking through this new property, Gary noticed several saplings of species that typically grow to great heights. These trees were rare in the mature La Selva old-growth forest, suggesting that they needed disturbance and full sun to survive. They took root only when a gap opened above a fallen seed or when a seed happened to end up in an existing gap. Gary thought that perhaps some of the rare La Selva tree species required the full sun of tree fall gaps in order to establish themselves. This led him down a whole new avenue of investigation that has since turned into its own discipline—gap ecology, or the study of tree falls and the forest areas they open.

When a tree comes crashing down, a new gap is created. Seeds lying on the forest floor or slightly buried beneath the soil are then newly exposed

Cleared areas are eventually filled in with new growth.
These two experimental plots at La Selva show the growth that
has occurred after one year (left) and two years (right).

to far more sunlight. In response to the increased light levels, germination takes place. In a few short years, the gap is colonized, filled in by a variety of fast-growing trees. Because of the competition for light with other plants, these young trees practically race each other to see who gets to the canopy first. Over the course of a three-year study, Gary determined that about one-half of the 320 species found in the La Selva forest require gaps to successfully establish the next generation of trees. At the time his study was conducted, most scientists then believed that there was very little change in tropical rain forests. They thought of them as stable, ancient plant communities where individual trees grew very slowly. Gary's groundbreaking research changed the way people think about tropical forests. It showed that the trees of the rain forest form a dynamic, or ever-changing, community. His findings also opened the door for many other research projects studying the role tree fall gaps play in the life of a forest.

In addition to his work with gap theory, Gary specializes in tropical dendrology. Dendrology is the study and identification of trees. His work

Much of the rain forest in South and Central America has been cleared and burned to provide pasture for cattle. Here only a few trees have been spared in this stretch of Costa Rican forest.

has focused on collecting botanical specimens and sending them off to specialists who determine the species' scientific names. Not surprisingly, some of the specimens Gary has sent turned out to be species scientists never knew existed. A number of specimens Gary has collected in Costa Rica and the Peruvian Amazon have been officially described as new species, including trees in both the avocado and mulberry families. In fact, in recognition of Gary's contributions to the field of tropical dendrology, a total of six new tree species are named after him. These include a giant tree at La Selva now known as *Ocotea hartshorniana* and one in Costa Rica's Braulio Carrillo National Park called *Macrolobium hartshornii*.

While working in the field, Gary became greatly concerned with the

Education has been an important part of Gary Hartshorn's mission throughout his career. Here he leads a workshop along a trail at the Explorama Lodge near the Amazon River in Peru.

destruction of tropical forests for the sale of timber and to create more pastureland for cattle. He believed that landowners needed other ways to make money so they would not have to cut down the valuable forest. So while working as a forestry consultant for the Tropical Science Center, Gary used his knowledge of tree fall gaps to develop a new way to manage tropical forests. What he proposed is known as the strip-cut method.

Using Gary's approach, loggers cut all the trees located on a long, narrow strip of forest and harvest all of its wood. The swaths cut were 100 to 130 feet (30–40 m) wide and repeated every 500 to 650 feet (153–198 m). These long clear-cut strips allowed sunlight to reach the forest floor and trigger the growth of thousands of seeds that were already in the soil or that were soon deposited by birds and bats. Gary worked with an Indian forestry cooperative in the Peruvian Amazon to test his new approach. The strip-cuts were soon filled with the seedlings of hundreds of native tree species. The full sun stimulated very rapid growth of these young trees. From an ecological point of view, Gary's strip-cut model for producing timber in tropical rain forests was a great success. Unfortunately, as with so many new ideas that differ from traditional techniques, this method has not been widely adopted in the rain forest. But Gary's method proves how valuable our study of the rain forest is. By understanding how this complex world works, we are better prepared to preserve and protect it.

At a field site near Puerto Maldonado, Peru, Terry Erwin prepares to use a crossbow to fire a line over a branch. This is the first step in moving his fogger into place. The fishing line shot from the crossbow can then be used to pull up a thicker cord.

Chapter Five

IN A FOG

T he roar of the fogger drones on. Large white plumes spew from the barrel, creating a billowy cloud that eventually fills the entire canopy at each station. Then, suddenly, the noisy contraption is switched off. Slowly the sounds of the forest return. The drip of moisture from leaves. The flutter of birds in the understory. And then the soft plops of small objects hitting the nylon trays. It has started to rain, but not water. The light shower of insects has begun.

The man who has turned off the fogger is Dr. Terry Erwin. The cloud he creates is really gas, poisonous only to arthropods—the class of organisms that includes insects and spiders. He has helped perfect a method of fogging the canopy that allows researchers to collect insects that would otherwise be out of reach. By using his fogger, Terry and his colleagues can collect specimens, or samples, from nearly the highest trees.

Dr. Erwin is a coleopterist—an entomologist who specializes in the study of beetles. The term comes from the name of the insect order, or group, that represents the beetles—the Coleoptera. Insects are divided into about thirty orders, but Coleoptera is by far the largest. This huge division is broken into smaller groups called families, one of which is the Carabidae, or ground beetles. It is the ground beetles that have held Dr. Erwin's main interest throughout his career.

In addition to being a coleopterist, Dr. Erwin is a taxonomist for the National Museum of Natural History at the Smithsonian Institution. As a taxonomist, he categorizes beetle specimens according to their character-

Weevils are the most abundant and diverse family of beetles. This one has several mites crawling on its legs and thorax. Terry Erwin has collected more than a thousand species of beetles from a single rainforest tree.

istics and anatomy, or body structure. He is especially interested in knowing all about ground beetles—or carabids as they are sometimes called—including how many species there are and how they relate to one another. It is part of his job to search out ground beetles, identify them, and describe the new species he finds.

Terry's ground beetle work brought him to the Smithsonian Tropical Research Institute (STRI) on Barro Colorado Island in Panama in the early

1970s. STRI is a community of scientists who live on the island and study all aspects of its plant and animal life. Among those working there at the time were an ecologist named Yael Lubin and a wildlife biologist named Gene Montgomery. They were interested in knowing how many termites and ants were available to anteaters in the treetops. In order to find out, the two scientists and Dr. Erwin experimented with devices that would release an insecticide in the top of a tree so that they could then collect the dead insects that fell to the ground.

Terry Erwin and a Peruvian coworker check equipment used for laying out a field plot. Attention to detail and a careful record of observations are necessary so that no valuable data are lost.

Just before dawn, after the nocturnal insects have gone to roost and before the diurnal insects have become active, Terry Erwin fogs a rainforest tree with a cloud of insecticide. The cooler pre-dawn air helps the insecticide to spread through the tree's crown. One of the devices used to capture the falling insects is seen on the left.

This was no easy task, as some of the trees on the mainland near the island were 100 to 120 feet (30.4–36.5 m) tall. In those days, the device had to be somehow hoisted into the tree. But most importantly, the release of the insecticide needed to be carefully controlled. The poison had to kill the insects, but not harm the birds, monkeys, and other canopy residents. Finally, the dead insects had to be collected from among the dense foliage beneath the target tree. These challenges are typical of those researchers face in the field.

Terry's fogger has gone through a lot of changes since those early days. Even today, working in Ecuador in the Amazon Basin, Terry continues to make adjustments and slight improvements. However, after years of successful collecting in the field, the basic approach has been set. First, a fogging design is prepared. This is done in advance when the chosen trees can be clearly seen. Various factors are considered such as the canopy height, whether trees stand alone or are touching, and whether the trees in the sampling area can be identified. If the trees meet all these requirements, the collecting devices included in the fogging design are placed in the forest with as little disturbance to the understory as possible. The collecting traps are most often nylon trays or aluminum funnels. In clearing the area, Dr. Erwin's team has even developed eco-friendly ways of cutting small plants so that they easily recover.

The insecticide used to kill the insects is called resmethrin. Once released it quickly takes effect. It is applied as a cloud of insecticide made by the bazooka-like fogger. The liquid insecticide is poured into a chamber, where it is released from the barrel as very fine particles that give it the appearance of white billowing smoke. An important property of this insecticide is that it breaks down very quickly in the environment without doing any harm.

Perhaps the hardest part of using the fogger is that it weighs 40 pounds (18.1 kg) and must be carried long distances from the camp to the study site each morning before dawn. Although the fogger can be hand held and used from ground level when the tree is small—30 feet (9.1 m) or less—in most cases the canopy area to be fogged is three times that height. In the early days of fogging, to get the fogger high into the treetops, Terry started with a thin strand of fishing line with a small weight attached to it. A device, such as a slingshot, a crossbow, or a launcher, is used to loop it over the highest branch large enough to support it. When the line is in place, its end is tied to a heavier and stronger cord that is then pulled up into the tree. This is repeated with heavier lines, until a rope capable of supporting the fogger is in place.

The fogger that Terry used in those days was equipped with radio controls. They allowed him to operate it from the ground. Once hoisted into position, Terry could guide the direction and angle of the barrel in order to send the fog through as much of the treetop as possible. Without the remote controls, a researcher would have to climb with ropes or spurs and direct the fogger by hand.

The fogging itself is typically done at dawn. There is little air movement then, and the air is somewhat cooler. At that time of day, the hot cloud of insecticide tends to rise and spread so that even greater area is covered in the fog. Prior to starting the fogger, collecting surfaces, much like a tarp, are tied to trees with strings. If aluminum funnels are used to collect the falling insects, they are secured with stakes to the ground. They both make it easier to see the insects when they fall, while also keeping them separate from the leaf litter on the forest floor.

A few minutes after the fogging is complete, insects and other invertebrates begin falling from the canopy. There is seldom a "downpour," unless a wasp or ant nest has been affected by the mist. Usually there is a steady "drizzle" of insects over the next two hours. Large heavy-bodied ones, such as beetles, grasshoppers, and katydids, can be heard striking the collecting surface before they tumble down the funnel-like device into a bottle of 75% alcohol. The lighter insects sometimes take a little longer to descend.

Terry has used this method to collect canopy specimens from throughout the Amazon Basin, including more than a dozen field sites in Brazil, Peru, and Ecuador. As a direct result of his work more than six million arthropods have been gathered, and the Smithsonian's collection now boasts more than a million ground beetles. Many of the specimens that make up this vast wealth are housed in the National Museum of Natural

Terry Erwin is a coleopterist, an entomologist who specializes in the study of beetles. Pictured here is a ground beetle, a member of the group Dr. Erwin knows best.

History, where specialists in various insect groups will continue to examine them for decades to come.

Terry's work has done much to change our thoughts about insect biodiversity on this planet. Before he began analyzing his fogging results, the total number of insect species was estimated at about 2 to 3 million. However, on one occasion, Terry collected more than 1,700 species from a single tree. Based on his new data and factoring in the number of different trees and forest types found throughout the world, Terry now estimates that there may be as many as 30 million species of insects.

Terry has trained numerous students and colleagues. Some of his peers have been conducting similar fogging studies using his same techniques in Africa, Malaysia, and areas of the Pacific. The combined information will allow researchers to compare insect life in different tropical regions around the world. Terry's groundbreaking work with canopy fogging has shown there is still much to be learned about the world around us.

Paul Donahue and Teresa
Wood pose on the walkway
from which they have
logged many hours
observing rainforest birds.

Chapter Six

BIRD'S-EYE VIEW

I f you love birds, the Amazon Basin is a great place to work. Paul Donahue and Teresa Wood are tropical ornithologists who have combined their daring and know-how to open up a whole new world for bird researchers and the curious visitor alike. Their interest in the lives of various species and their desire to tape-record the vocalizations, or songs, of birds led them up into the trees. Birds also serve as the greatest inspiration for Paul's painting. Using their special knowledge of climbing and canopy access, they have built in the treetops a series of walkways and observation platforms at various rain-forest sites. Through their company Treetop Explorations, they survey, plan, and build the structures that allow tourists and scientists without climbing skills to access the canopy.

Bird life in the rain forest is stratified. That means that for feeding and roosting, each species generally prefers one of the forest's many layers. Living at different heights in the trees is an adaptation that leads to decreased competition for food and space. Some birds are found only at ground level, like the tinamou and red-billed ground cuckoo. Others frequent only the understory, such as the collared trogon, blue-crowned mot mot, and the long-tailed hermit. Among the residents of the lower and upper parts of the canopy are macaws, toucans, oropendolas, and parrots. Up at the top of the forest are the tallest emergent trees, thick with vegetation and reaching 175 feet (53.3 m). That makes it very difficult for

After years of practice, Paul Donahue can move through the trees like a monkey. But it is always a good idea to have a safety rope in place.

an observer on the ground to identify what birds live there, much less study their behavior and natural history.

The trees are also host to some complex partnerships. Many insectivorous, or insect-eating, birds in tropical forests live in permanent groupings known as mixed-species flocks. These bands of birds lay claim to territories that they defend from other rival flocks. This teamwork is another strategy for increasing the birds' chances of survival. Some of these flocks forage in the undergrowth and understory of the forest. Others prefer the canopy. While certain species are commonly found in almost all of the flocks, other less common or rare species appear only in a few. These are of particular interest to researchers.

Paul and Teresa first used small observation platforms at the Explorer's Inn in the Tambopata-Candamo Reserve of southeastern Peru. Not used to seeing people in the treetops, birds approached much more closely than they did at ground level, especially if a fruiting tree was nearby. Paul was able to observe and sketch at close range many bird species he had previously known only as tiny specks in the canopy above him. He was able to make the first tape recordings of a few canopy bird species such as the black-faced hawk and white-browed purpletuft. Teresa became the first person to find and describe the nest of the beautiful paradise tanager. Being on high certainly had its advantages. And since the movements of individual birds and flocks could be tracked over far greater distances than from the forest floor, estimates of territory size were much easier to make.

Airborne Ants

One of the more unusual discoveries Paul made early in his canopy work involved not birds but ants. Almost every tree he climbed at the Tambopata-Candamo Reserve seemed to be swarming with one of two large ant species, *Campanotus sericeiventris* and *Cephalotes atratus*. For a canopy worker, both species were equally a nuisance. The *Campanotus* would bite if you accidentally touched it. While the *Cephalotes* did not bite, you could still get pricked by the sharp projections on the back of their flattened heads. Since these ants were very common, even abundant, and since constantly getting pricked wasn't fun, Paul began brushing them off the limbs where he was working. However, he soon noticed that no matter how hard he flicked the ants and regardless of the direction in which he sent them, only rarely would the ants fall to the ground. They would typically descend 20 to 30 feet (6.1–9.1 m), then adjust the course of their fall and sail right back in towards the trunk of the tree.

When Paul realized this, he began experimenting, dropping ants farther and farther away from the trunk of the tree. Even 10 feet (3 m) from the trunk, the *Cephalotes* were still able to correct their course and glide back toward the tree. Only about one ant in ten would appear to fall all the way to the ground. Why? Paul looked to the ants wide, aerodynamic heads for the answer. They seem to be able to use their unusually shaped heads as a parachute or a hang glider to "fly," or at least to change their path and avoid falling. This proved to be a very important adaptation for both a canopy creature and a colonial animal dependent on its sister ants for survival.

Walking in the Treetops

The longer Teresa and Paul worked in the canopy, the more they wished there was some easy way to travel from tree to tree, rather than having to sit and wait for the birds and other wildlife to come to them. So, they began to map out the route for a possible canopy walkway. Funding its construction, however, was another matter, and they had little success finding a backer.

Then in late 1991 they were asked to help with the construction of a canopy walkway at the Amazon Center for Environmental Education and Research, near the Rio Napo in northeastern Peru. Eventually, Paul and Teresa took over as the directors, supervising a local crew of workers. The walkway was completed in April 1994.

The ACEER Canopy Walkway, the world's longest, is 1,475 feet (450 m)

*The paradise tanager frequents the canopy where it searches
for insects and fruits. Its bright plumage has earned it the name
siete çolores, which in Spanish means "seven colors." Teresa was
the first person to document the nest of this elusive species.*

long and 120 feet (36.5 m) above the ground at its highest point. It connects thirteen large, emergent trees, with one or two observation platforms in each tree. The walkway is basically a series of aluminum ladders that are bolted end to end and hung from steel cables by ropes threaded through the hollow rungs of the ladders. Planks are placed on top of the rungs to make it easier to walk. Safety netting lines the path up to about shoulder level. In building the walkway, great care was taken to make

Teresa Wood checks a rope as she stands on part of the
canopy walkway she helped build at the Amazon Center
for Environmental Education and Research (ACEER).

sure the environment was not harmed. The route was carefully chosen to avoid having to prune any large branches or limbs. The support trees were all well braced, and below the walkway the paths used by the workers were protected with wooden steps to prevent erosion. The walkway is now being used for tourism, research, and environmental education and receives approximately 2,000 visitors each year.

For a bird-watcher, the walkway is a great success. It wraps around the tallest hill in the area, winding in and out of the canopy. It offers access to birds that prefer the shade of the forest interior, such as the chestnut-winged hookbill, as well as to those preferring the open sunlight like the white-necked puffbird. The walkway also includes almost the entire territory of the largest canopy mixed-species flock in the area. More than eighty-five species of birds have been seen foraging with the flock at one time or another. The flock can be located on almost every trip to the canopy. With luck it can be followed for most of the day, providing a whole new look into the workings of these canopy associations. Small canopy birds such as ash-winged antwrens and white-bellied dacnis, previously hardly known, can now be observed at close range for long periods.

Paul and Teresa are currently beginning a project to construct a 1-mile-long (1,524-m) canopy walkway at Manu Wildlife Center in southeastern Peru. While their first two canopy walkways were owned by commercial tour operators, this walkway will be owned by the Asociacion para la Conservacion de la Selva Sur (Selva Sur, for short), a conservation group based in Cuzco, Peru. It will be used for ecotourism, and the proceeds will be used to finance conservation projects and protect more rain forest. When completed the walkway will be more than three times as long as the ACEER Canopy Walkway, connecting about forty emergent trees. It will be located in a large private reserve along the Rio Madre de Dios, a short distance downstream of the Manu Biosphere Reserve. The area hosts jaguars, more than 10 species of monkeys, and of course birds—more than 550 species—including harpy eagles, guans, curassows, and a

Macaws are among the largest species of parrots that
forage for fruit in the canopy. Pairs of blue-and-gold macaws
such as these are common sights from the walkway.

wealth of large macaws. In most parts of the Amazon Basin, these species have grown scarce. As the rain forest continues to be developed and cut down, their habitats are shrinking more and more. Thus the reserve and the walkway that threads through part of it are vital to protecting and studying these threatened species.

Paul and Teresa are actively involved in conservation efforts to preserve forests in both North and South America. They believe that the tropical rain forest, as well as the rest of the planet, is in very serious trouble. They also feel it is especially important to teach young people about the value of the earth's natural resources and the challenges we face. For that reason, both of them have spent a great deal of time, not only in the rainforest canopy, but in classrooms back in the United States.

GETTING STARTED

How do you make that first step to get from your home to the Amazon jungle? How do you know if a job in the rain forest is right for you? For the budding scientist or the eager adventurer, these are important questions. Fortunately, you do not have to wait until you are in college, as many of the scientists described in this book did. Now more than ever, there are opportunities for young people to visit the Amazon and experience the wonders of a tropical forest firsthand.

ECOTOURS

One way to get a brief look at a rainforest habitat is by participating in a natural history tour. Many companies offer environmentally sensitive tours, or ecotours, to rainforest sites in countries such as Peru, Ecuador, Venezuela, Brazil, and Costa Rica. Such brief trips are a wonderful introduction to tropical travel, especially if you do not speak Spanish or Portuguese. With planned itineraries and professional guides, these programs, which usually last from one to two weeks, allow participants to make their own observations of the complex world of rain forests.

CHILDREN'S ENVIRONMENTAL TRUST FOUNDATION, INTERNATIONAL

The Children's Environmental Trust Foundation, International (CET) brings middle school, high school, and college students from the United States to tropical forest sites in Peru, Costa Rica, and Brazil to teach them about the rain forest. The mission of CET is not only to provide its participants with an exciting experience in a spectacular setting, but to expose students to the complex issues of rainforest conservation and destruction.

ORGANIZATION FOR TROPICAL STUDIES

The Organization for Tropical Studies (OTS) trains college students in all aspects of tropical biology and ecology through offering diverse courses at field stations in Costa Rica, Peru, and Brazil. Classes are available to both U.S. and Latin American students, and instruction is conducted in either English or Spanish depending on the course.

EARTHWATCH INSTITUTE

The Earthwatch Institute has been crucial in supporting research of natural history topics, including rain forests as well as many other subjects, for more than twenty-five years. Their unique approach is to obtain funding for projects by finding volunteers who perform field research and pay for the experience with a pre-determined donation that covers the expenses of the project.

GLOSSARY

aerodynamic: specially designed to fly or glide through the air.

alternative medicine: any method of treating an illness, including herbal remedies, that differs from traditional practices.

arthropod: a group of organisms, including insects and spiders, characterized by having jointed legs.

biodiversity: the variety of living things within a certain area or ecosystem.

canopy: the part of a rain forest formed by the crowns of its tallest trees.

clear-cut: a timber practice where all the trees in a given area are harvested.

coleopterist: an entomologist who studies beetles.

colonial: living in groups, such as with the social insects bees, wasps, ants, and termites.

competition: the state when two or more organisms or species inhabit the same area and use the same resources.

curandero: a native healer or medicine man.

echolocation: process by which some bats locate their prey and guide their flight by sending out sounds and then listening for and interpreting their echoes as they bounce off objects.

ecologist: a scientist who studies ecology or the relationships of organisms to their environment.

emergent: the tallest of rainforest trees whose crowns stick up and above the canopy.

entomologist: a scientist who studies insects.

ethnobotanist: a scientist who studies plants and how they are used by groups of people.

frugivory: having a diet that consists of fruit.

germination: process by which a seed sprouts and gives rise to a seedling.

habitat: physical area in which an organism lives.

herbarium: a collection of plant specimens that are identified and used as references.

insecticide: a poison used to kill insects.

insectivorous: having a diet that consists of insects.

mammalogist: a scientist who studies mammals.

mark-recapture study: a scientific investigation where the target organisms are captured, marked in some manner so that they can be identified, released, and then observed or trapped again.

mixed-species flock: a group of different species of birds that forage together to decrease competition and increase their hunting success.

organism: a living creature.

ornithologist: a scientist who studies birds.

sonar: process of locating objects by using sound waves and their echoes.

stratified: having multiple layers.

strip-cut: method of timber harvesting where narrow rows of trees are cut leaving the forest standing on either side.

taxonomist: a scientist who studies a particular group of organisms and classifies them into categories so that they can be identified.

undergrowth: the shrub and ground layer of plants that grows beneath the understory.

understory: small and medium-sized trees that can grow in the shade whose crowns form the layer between the canopy and the undergrowth.

FIND OUT MORE

BOOKS

Castner, James L. *Explorama's Amazon.* Gainesville, FL: Feline Press, 2000.

Davis, Wade. *One River.* New York: Touchstone Books, 1996.

Duke, James A. *The Green Pharmacy.* New York: St. Martin's Press, 1997.

Goodman, Susan E. *Bats, Bugs, and Biodiversity.* New York: Antheneum Books for Young Readers, 1995.

Lasky, Kathryn. *The Most Beautiful Roof in the World.* San Diego: Gulliver Green/Harcourt Brace & Company, 1997.

Plotkin, Mark J. *Tales of a Shaman's Apprentice.* New York: Penguin Books, 1993.

Wilson, Don, and Ruff, Sue. *Bats.* New York: Benchmark Books, 2001.

WEBSITES

Amazon Conservation Team
www.ethnobotany.org

Father Nature's Farmacy
www.ars-grin.gov/duke

Treetop Explorations
www.nemaine.com/treetopexplorations

Amazonarium
www.amazonarium.com.br

Smithsonian Institution
www.si.edu

American Museum of Natural History
www.amnh.org

Field Museum of Natural History
www.fmnh.org

ORGANIZATIONS

Organization for Tropical Studies
Box 90630
Durham, NC 27708-0630
(919) 684-5774
www.ots.duke.edu

Children's Environmental Trust, International
201 W. Main
Zeeland, MI 49464
(888) 748-9993
www.cetfoundation.org

Earthwatch Institute
3 Clock Tower Place, Suite 100
Box 75
Maynard, MA 01754
(800) 776-0188
www.earthwatch.org

Bat Conservation International
P.O. Box 162603
Austin, TX 78716
(512) 327-9721
www.batcon.org

American Botanical Council
P.O. Box 144345
Austin, TX 78714-4345
(512) 926-4900
www.herbalgram.org

All Species
727A Liggett Avenue
San Francisco, CA 94129
(415) 776-1555
www.all-species.org

ABOUT THE AUTHOR

Dr. James L. Castner is a tropical biologist-writer-photographer and adjunct professor of biology at Pittsburg State University. He has traveled throughout the rain forests of South and Central America, but has focused primarily on the Amazon Basin of Peru. His main interest is how insects defend themselves, especially with the use of camouflage and mimicry. His unique photos of rainforest insects have appeared in *National Geographic*, *Natural History*, *International Wildlife*, *Ranger Rick*, and *Kids Discover* magazines.

Dr. Castner has spent the past several years writing books about insects and the rain forest. He often conducts educational workshops and leads students and teachers on visits to the Tropics. As part of his desire to work with younger students, he is completing his secondary certification in science and Spanish. He plans to finish his career teaching a combination of middle school, high school, and college students.

INDEX